MW00698067

Book Design
  Benjamin Daniel Lawless, Penciled In

 Solo Press
5146 Foothill Road
Carpinteria, CA 93013
solopress.org

ISBN-13: 978-0-941490-43-6

FOOT SOLDIER

NEW AND SELECTED POEMS

by

John Stevens Berry

By John Stevens Berry

Poetry:
Darkness of Snow

Prose:
Those Gallant Men (Vietnam Memoir)
The Twelfth Victim
    Co-authored with Linda Battisti

Acknowledgments

Thanks to the Academy of American Poets
for awards given for some of these poems,
and for inclusion of poems in an anthology
compiled by Louise Bogan.

Thanks to the Presidio Press, the Military Book Club,
Café Solo, The New Mexico Quarterly, Hyperion,
Sequoia, and The Stanford Daily, where some
of these poems have appeared, and to the
John H. Ames reading series, and to Larksong,
for filming the reading of some of these poems.

Introduction
by Roger Welsch

> "In battle men fall
> > By saber and sword,
> But no blade is sharper
> > Than that of the word."

— George Schwelle, *Metrics*, Canto IV, rime 7

Poetry, contrary to a couple centuries of error, is the language of warriors. From marching "Jodies" to Samoan Hakas, from Viking skalds to chivalric bards, from lays to chansons, flyting to "slams," the art of language has been celebrated in the poetry of conflict, sometimes as inspiration — sometimes as substitute.

I can imagine that some who know John Stevens Berry as a Rabelesian rouser, a man as fully content as an agitator where calm would otherwise reign, or perhaps a solemn barrister in the model of Horace Rumpole, might be flummoxed by the notion of him as, of all things, a poet! But I would argue that if I knew nothing of J.S. other than his work in the courts, I would wonder why he was not composing poetry. He is a master of language as surely as he is a master of jurisprudence.

The poets in my life have been more like J.S. "Mad Dog" Berry than Ernie Kovacs's Percy Dovetonsils: Bill Kloefkorn, Jim Harrison, John Neihardt, Bunky EchoHawk... Warriors... poets. Indeed, our mutual friend and late Nebraska State Poet, Bill Kloefkorn, wrote of Berry, "In an age of froth and whimsy, Berry gives us poems made of iron. He is a demanding poet. His poems require close listening, rather than mere skimming. Sometimes he assumes that the reader is familiar with classical antiquity. In short, he breaks all the contemporary rules. But his poems are strong and true. That still counts for something."

Yes, Bill, indeed it does.

Dannebrog, Nebraska
May 17, 2022

Roger Welsch was a folklorist and author of over 40 books including *Touching the Fire* and *The Reluctant Pilgrim*.

For Margaret

After 50 years

Mostly, our lives are made up of small moments.
My mother said
She brings a sense of occasion.
A wealth of moments.

Our wars were different, but the same.
I was a captain in III Corps.
You were a novice
in a convent.

Neither of us saved the world.
We both wear bruises
that glow in the dark.

Once my gunship flew low over a roof
with an astonishing painted eye —
eternal, all-seeing, Cao Dai.

Your brown eyes break war's gaze,
and lead me to your art, coloring the moments
that give shape and shade to life.

TABLE OF CONTENTS

PART 1
FOOT SOLDIER

PART 2
ONAWA

PART 3
PERSONAE

PART 4
MYTHOS

PART 5

DARKNESS OF SNOW

PART 1

FOOT SOLDIER

The Platte, Not the Mekong

Not a four acre farm to provide one meal a day.
Just the flash and blaze of lightning and a hay stack.
Still, I slap leather which isn't there
for my pistol which isn't there,
for reassurance, which, for a split second,
isn't there.

Corn fields, not rice paddies.
Steel irrigation systems, not *ba gia*
with her ancient legs walking in place
on treadles, and handle arms made of bamboo
to move water.

After war, you are never quite
where you belong.

Paternal

Stained, worn,
my dad's World War I greatcoat,
smelling of damp old wool,
hung in the basement.

He did not live long enough
to hear about my war

so I never got to tell him
about kerosene-fueled burning shit
or rotting bodies amid the diesel.

He wanted his boys to be officers.
Said where there were outhouses,
	the enlisted lines were long.
Officers got right in.

And he told me the best smell
was bending to kiss a sleeping child:
sweat, wind, sun, and child hair.

Easter Sunday, 1969

Angel Wing Cambodian border.

Brief fight.

Other guy dies.

Is that Easter?

Do we live because someone bled?

Don't know.

But it brings a man to his knees.

Danse Macabre

He plays his fiddle
or the VC bugle
we found among bodies.
And corpses leap forth

from graves
or body bags,
some sitting up
in cadaveric spasm.

Corpses fart and groan.
Crucifixion gives "angel lust" erections.
Dead women have coffin birth,
gas forcing the fetus out.

Shall we dance?
Snappy little tap dance?

Too old to die young,
I choose tango,
sarabande—hell, polka—
if I'm really lucky.

But, yeah, waltz clog,
shuffle ball change.
The fucking dance
goes on.

Beggars Beads

In McCook, Nebraska, Kay
got herself entangled
with a married couple.

Couldn't get out.
Got her parents involved.
Gentle folk, I knew them all, who were rewarded
by getting shot, sawed up,
wrapped in butcher paper, and dumped
into Strunk Lake.

Come spring, a lucky angler
hooked a human breast.
It put up no fight at all.

War memories surface like that,
unbidden. How in Saigon, I bought
my mother beggars beads.
Worthless rocks
strung together
as best some guy could.

The Cao Dai Temple
at Tay Ninh.
Maybe a half million members.
Turns out Confucianism, Taoism, Buddhism
are one.

Victor Hugo and Sun Yat Sen
are venerable saints,
and Joan of Arc
fits in.

Incense offering, prayer
to the Jade Emperor—
who is God the Father, after all—
and the three jewels:
flower, wine, and tea.

At Fire Base Saint Barbara,
we shelled Nui Ba Den,
the Black Virgin Mountain,
but their goddess
outlasted our saint.

Angel wing of the Cambodian border,
my blade beat another.
An eruption of blood
all over my shirt.

Stripped down.

Bac-si, medic, said,

"Lucky guy, Cap. That's someone else's blood."

Every fucking drop.

Permissive Travel Orders

I could go anywhere.
Bribed my way into the Emperor's Study in Hue,
went off limits to the Cao Dai Temple in Nha Trang,

all four Corps Areas of Operation.
Once, a young lieutenant was trying to get me
onto a chopper. They were loading body bags.

"The captain has permissive travel orders."
The bored specialist nodded at the body bags.
"Yeah, these guys got 'em too."

Foot Soldier

for J.F.

In Basic, Larry spit shined his boots.
Polish, a cloth, spit, even a little aftershave lotion.
His platoon sergeant said, "You could shave by that!"

Larry explained that these were his first new shoes.
He did not need cardboard to cover holes.
So he polished, patiently.
They were perfect.

Later, in Afghanistan, he saw corn planted by hand.
Kids followed, barefoot, tiny feet
pressing seeds into the earth.

A mine.
The docs at the NATO Hospital in Kabul used 18 screws
to save the foot and ankle.

Back in the World,
he said he wouldn't take the pain—
agreed to amputation,
but wanted to keep his foot and ankle.

Honey and aspic embalmed, carefully and
        tirelessly polished.
And when he married, he had his foot and ankle there,
in a glass case.
Married body and soul.

I nod,
exalted by the marriage of foot, seed, and earth,
limp away,
grateful for my VA cane.

Fire

Kim Phuc:
they call you "napalm girl."
9 years old,

playing in a temple
(where you thought you must be safe)
when your own country

laid flaming napalm.
Your village, Trang Bang;
bodies in flames.

So you ran.
Tore off your burning clothes,
and a soldier gave you a sip,

then poured his canteen over you
and you blacked out,
but not before you had been photographed

naked as a grandchild,
naked as hunger,
naked as fear,

naked as death.

Operation Ranch Hand

Sounds wholesome—
Guys who kept livestock healthy and fed,
maybe oversaw breeding.

So some pencilneck at the Pentagon
decided it would be a good name
for herbicidal warfare,

and the clever motto:
"only you can prevent forests."

Body count was a big deal,
and so were other stats:

20,000,000 gallons of defoliant
on rural areas, deprived VC
of food and vegetation cover.

5,000,000 acres of forest,
500,000 acres of crops,
the spraying from C-123 s,
call sign "Hades."

Agent Orange.
And green, pink, purple, blue, white:
a war of color code names.

And if no pencilneck cares
about the wildlife that lost their habitat,
are they at least interested in 150,000
Vietnamese children with severe birth defects?

They do know the VA has cancers,
heart disease, Parkinson's and diabetes
to pay for.

Oh yeah, spina bifida can be passed on
to a soldier's kids. Real money here.

Operation Ranch Hand.
Well, a good hand is set for slaughter.

Sycamore

Behind my grandparents' house,
between the storm cellar
and my grandmother's acres of peonies,

the iron pump.
The water smelled, tasted like iron.

Farther from the house,
in the firefly dark
I held a girl,

a lovely girl
who smelled of a young sycamore
after a spring rain.

They say the VC could smell
where we had passed.

No aftershave, of course,
and days without soap or detergent.
But they could smell us.

If we smell different,
blood smells the same:
rust.

No iron pump,
no sycamore.
Just rust.

Story

Seven years before Nha Trang:
1961, Fort Leonard Wood, Missouri;
I was a second lieutenant,
pushing troops through Basic.

The base stunk of coal furnaces,
and the major's wife knew
just the girl for me.

18, a beautician, dark hair
the girl lived in Plato,
south gate to the post.

She attended the Church of God,
and told me it was wrong to sing in church.
She smelled of soap, and was anxious
      to get her heart broken.

One day a bunch of lieutenants
decided on a different kind of Saturday night.
We would not have a steak at the officers club,
or risk a fight on the strip,
or visit whatever girl the major's wife
      may have found for us.

Nope. Going to East St. Louis.
Ribs, jazz, bet the ponies at Kahokia Downs.
We were making $200 a month,
no reason not to go a little crazy.

I was Officer of the Day Friday, so I would start late
and meet the guys at the Track.

But I got lost.

Pulled into a small town.

In the square: a country fiddlers contest.
Some old guy selling nickel popcorn,
fireflies, barefoot kids, an empty park bench.

From the bench the respectful silence
for good fiddle music.
The people were welcoming or not.

A sense of inclusion and otherness
brought me somewhere I had never been,
but that I had missed, and acutely.
Universe made right for the moment.

The judge wore a gown and bonnet.
She chose the winner; they played
Arkansas Traveler together. She curtsied, he bowed.

I could not speak, just went back to the post.
Sometimes only silence works.

Seven years later, among dead Vietcong,
the helmet revealed a dark haired girl,
maybe 18, maybe a little like the girl
            whose heart I had chosen not to break.

And only silence worked.

The Call

PTSD Brother. Triggered. Ukraine invasion.

I say *I know.*
I say *Got your 6.*
He wants to pray. Okay.

But I know.
101st Airborne, Hamburger Hill.
Screaming Eagles.
"Rendezvous with destiny."

May, 1968, I was klicks away from the A Shau Valley,
West of Hue,
Near Laos.

Operation Apache Snow.
Ap Bia, "the mountain of the crouching beast."
Double and triple canopy jungle,
frontal attack.

He speaks of body bags, medevac dustoffs,
mostly of his buddy Copeland,
suddenly with no left arm, blood spurting
until it and his life stopped.

We took the hill,
  then abandoned it.
"Some fucking rendezvous with destiny," he says.

Then he asks if we can pray.
We do.

Ars Moriendi

Inscribed
on my dad's World War I Victory Medal:
The war to end all wars

And on the black wall:
the name of my cousin:
Johnny Stevens

On my dog tags:
Protestant, A positive blood type.

Is there an art of dying?
A good death?
An absolution?

Who tells a soldier the very names
of those he left to rot?

And when Santayana tells us
only the dead have seen the end of war,
who cares if he stole that from Plato?

Who gives a rusty fuck
that boys hear the drum
and get pretty good
at the art of killing

unless, maybe
the end of war
is not a ghoulish taunt.

Fire Barrel

Fort Leonard Wood.
A big rusted barrel—
its flames gave us some warmth in snow.
Saw one just like it

as we left the freedom bird,
the big silver dustoff
that brought us back to the World.

Bottles of gut-wrecking
malaria pills,
orange dynamite.
We were to take them for a month.

The barrel stood by the landing strip,
and everyone tossed their pills into it.
Shedding part of the war,
a different kind of warming.

Foreign Claims

To pay a Vietnamese national,
loss must be collateral,
not combat related.

As if anything wasn't related
to everything
in this fucking war.

So: about $40 in piasters,
solatium for the 15 year-old kid you lost,
& a certificate & a bag of rice

& a bag with cigarettes and candy.
& that's all we could do.
All. We. Could. Do.

William Blake

My tiger was very different.
Not burning bright,
but seen briefly,

and not in the forests of the night.
Daytime rain forest outside Quang Tri.
Dark, stealthy of course, a sunlit patch

almost hidden by ferns and canopy trees.
We had automatic weapons,
but those few seconds scared hell out of me.

Did he who made the lamb
make Arc Light strikes?
Could an archangel destroy

everything for a mile long, a half mile wide,
as the Arc Light strike of 3 B-52 Bombers,
each carrying 60,000 pounds of bombs?

Hell firing down on people, huts, chickens, rice?
Did he smile his work to see?
Did he who made the lamb make me?

When the stars threw down their spears
and watered Heaven with their tears—

The two million candlepower parachute flares
dropped from the Douglas AC-47 Spooky flights,
Puff the Magic Dragon as the troops called them,

3 port side mini guns
that could fire 100 rounds per second,
hit every square yard of a football field in 10 seconds,

every fifth bullet a glowing red tracer
angelic or demonic across the night,
covering fire or suppressive fire,

depending on the color of the bodies.
So tell us:
When the stars throw down their spears
and water Heaven with their tears,

does Lucifer win?
Someone I trust tells me
there are maybe three tigers left alive in Vietnam.

There Will Be Cookies

Sam Hamai ran the Palo Alto Judo Club.
He wanted us to show up
and get hell beat out of us by the
    San Jose Buddhist team.
His pep talk: "*There will be cookies!*"

Of course I lost.
No flying ballet,
just grappling on the mat,
observing ancient courtesies.

The guy who beat me
gently explained why
I should have won.

Ten years later, Fire Base Tracey,
LZ Sam Houston, a probing action.
I had emptied the clips to my 1911 Colt .45.
He advanced on me, AK-47 ready.

I threw my pistol at his head.
Pissed him off, so he decided on his bayonet.
I deflected, a move Sam had taught me.
The Gerber Dirk, drawn from beneath my blouse

turned him into a red geyser.

Some asshole tried to photograph the body.
I punched the lieutenant's camera into his face.
A small courtesy, privacy in the humiliation of death.

In the Army you never
say goodbye. If you lose someone, you'll
see them on "the other side." Or, some say,
eternal fighting in Valhalla, mead and boar meat.

Don't know, of course, but I suspect
no golden harps, no halos,
no lounging on clouds.

No cookies, Sam,
but maybe something.
Maybe the best C-rations.
Canned peaches with pound cake.
How lucky can you get?

New Year's Eve, 1968.

My former wife
(now dead)
and her lover
(deader'n hell)
doubtless popped champagne.

Maybe in Tiburon,
perhaps Sausalito.
I was elsewhere.

Beyond Blackhorse, Xuan Loc
and Rock Village,
in a smaller town north

I had a hearing on a shooting;
the villagers
loved *dai uy map.*

Applauded my every gesture,
and booed the interpreter,
drinking coke

in my makeshift courtroom.
One client
(found not guilty)

gave me his pin:
Wine, women, bodycount.
At Firebase Tiger

my head was split and stitched.
My hooch maid scraped the blood
off my pillow, said

"V. C. numba ten."
Drunk in Saigon
I march to my hotel

singing "Georgie Girl"
late in a dark street,
weeks before Tet.

Other Veterans, Other Wars

Annual VA physical.
They have found me 290% disabled!
Of course they stop paying at 100%...

And I drove here by myself,
need a cane, of course, but still.

Scroomall, except six men to carry the box,
one road guard,
and one son of a bitch to count cadence.

But it does not take six to carry an urn,
no road guard or cadence at
     First Plymouth Columbarium.
Scroomall except

Bill Hart, Bob Jones, Wilford Heaton,
Robert Berry, Beech Dale, Saki Posz,
Lee Brumley, Bob Rheault, Larry Boyles,
Jack Crouchet, Johnny Stevens...

Yep, six feet of American earth, bought and paid for.
To dust they have returned.

In the 40s, Walt Andersen killed a German soldier
with his bare hands,
under a bridge, and under Patton.
Had headaches the rest of his life.

John Boosalis crashed in the Pacific, made it to shore.
Was rescued after there had already
     been a funeral for him.
I bowed my head at his next funeral.

Bill O fought at Bastogne. "They've got us surrounded,
     the poor bastards."
His story: a German family was kind to him.
So he stole a pound of butter and took it to the mother,
     who collapsed in sobs.

My three sons tell me nothing of Iraq and Afghanistan.

For all my PTSD and Agent Orange, I am
just another veteran, another war.

Les Jeux Sont Faites

Nope, sorry Baudelaire,
game ain't over,
still more bets.

My card deck:
Death from Above
airborne insignia with a skull.

Yup, psy ops gave them out.
Got mine at Redcatcher,
82nd Airborne forward base camp.

Sorry about your ennui.
I had another Charlie to kill,
rather as you killed time.

You liked Poe's Raven.
How about the VC skull in my study?
Would that cure your boredom?

We left cards on dead VC.
In French fortune telling tradition,
the Ace of Spades meant death.

Lots of GIs kept that card in their helmet band,
maybe had it tattooed
on their 18 year-old biceps.

Me? I kept the Queen of Hearts,
the fifth card in the Dead Man's Hand.
Don't display it like the skull,
but I still have it, somewhere.

Virgin Birth

of fog and mist

Suong means of the fog.
As a girl's name, "Dew."
Misty means misty.

Suong and Misty never met, but they were close—
geographically, and in their dark hair and eyes.

Suong was a nurse at Duster Compound.
Misty was a Red Cross worker out of II Field Force.
Off duty, in her neighborhood,
       Suong did what she could.

Suong was a nurse midwife
       among other skills and duties.
Nobody cared that she took what she needed
from her unit. For her people.

Misty went where her duties took her,
including the top of the Black Virgin.
"Surly tekkies" she called the Signal Corps
       troops stuck there—

dark, cloudy, on a hill owned by the VC.
Once, landing on the helipad,
she found a woman writhing in childbirth.

Misty held her shoulders, comforted her,
told her to push...
doing what she could

as Suong did every day, for her own people.

Mist, fog, dew — precursors
of total dark.

La Canción Feliz

Festival!
Some my age,
some mere children in their 70s.

A guy who was a squad leader
with the 9th,
ass deep in the Mekong

pulled his brother out of a burning tank.
Now Chuck has a bullet in his chest,
inoperable, moving toward his heart.

But he did okay.
Senator, Secretary of Defense,
Chuck addresses us.

Makes the silver spades, hard hats,
and blabbing politicians
tolerable.

A girl, maybe 11,
startling blue eyes,
braids, says

Grandpa,
what does it feel like to kill someone?
The same eyes,

a hand gentle on her back,
he whispers,
It don't.

Spectrum

"The difference between deadly force and lethal force,"
  expert witness says:
"Lethal force is worse."

 How?
Well, it seems deadly force *could* kill you.
Lethal force does.

 Rockets, mortars,
AK-47 fire, grenades
were deadly as hell,
but I'm still here.

And what of the River Lethe?
Well, you're already dead,
  and if you drink of the Lethe,
  you forget it all.
Clean slate for the next incarnation.

Nope. Sipping may help for a while,
but, as a corporal told me,
about a week before I saw him die,
This shit ain't goin nowhere.

That's Lethal shit.

Glass

Small, but fine legs. She walked me to her door.
I asked if the door mirror was to ward off dragons.
That's what they told us. A dragon would see its
    reflection and leave:
the house had its dragon.

That sad half smile. She was a nurse
    at Duster Compound.
Racist of me to think she would believe in dragons.
She tended to GIs who had been torn up,
like me, but in different ways.

Perfect English and French, and she helped me struggle
with an occasional Vietnamese phrase.
Colonial French blended into her features.
She was, Sergeant Maschmeier said, "pure class."

So she explained that the mirror was to
    deflect bad energy.
Death carries a fatal hourglass.
They used to hold a mirror to detect breathing
among the dead and dying.

And I have seen sealed coffins with glass windows
      to show the face.
What became of you, Miss Suong?
Re-education camp? Are you alive, maybe
somewhere in my country?

De Profundis

For J.J.S.

A pair to draw to, Sheila says.
Spanky and I sit at the bar.
He says nothing.

I shrug. Sheila lines them up.
Three shots for him.
I have my usual.

September 19. Another anniversary.
Over a half century ago,
gunship shot down;

he saw three crew mates burn.
Night sweats. His wife tells him
he throws things around the bedroom, not quite awake.

We sip. He says nothing.
Then, slowly,
"I drowned when I was six."

A neighbor farmer, not a friend,
was there, rolled him on a barrel,
forcing water out, reviving him.

I say nothing. Football:
farm work had made him tougher than the townies.
He loved to tackle.

No senior year for him.
Went to Mount St Michael's.
Didn't become a priest.

Engaged when he went off
to be a door gunner
and lost his friends.

Lost the girl, too.
Of course.
We say nothing.

Later, on my porch.
He needs to go home.
We bump fists. Enough said.

Makeout Bunker

They say *Even a Saigon whore*
insists on a bed with clean sheets.
Of course.

But war is not fastidious.
And sometimes,
when you can't get to Saigon,

or use the colonel's trailer,
this dark bunker,
set back a little from the others,

will have to do.
Sandbags, dirt, some worn canvas,
and a moment;

the chance to touch something soft
amid the sounds and smells
of war, sex, and love, this gift.

Smiles

When we were back at the barracks
and not sleeping under a sandbagged culvert half,
boots on, harms way,

we sipped, of course.
Called ourselves The Drugstore:

humor we had in store.
Pulaski had left part of an elbow
in the Central Highlands.

Reddington had been a philosophy major
and wanted to know
about Mike's 'Yard bracelet,

about the 30 tribes,
the six major ones,
mostly the Rade.

Wanted to know customs and
folklore and fighting techniques.
Why the women don't cover tits.

And the teeth: filed to a point,
kept black by chewing betel nuts.
About crossbows and courage.

Mike said this:
When Death smiles at a Montagnard,
the 'Yard smiles back.

Penang Lawyer

Impish Helen gave it to me.
Palm walking stick,
ornate knob.

She said it represented
rough justice,
could be used

to kill courtroom enemies.
She, a Donut Dollie
whose dad was a lawyer,

Wisconsin girl.
Lost track of her
like so many others.

The Sherlockian cane,
sweet souvenir
from a very long walk.

The Ice Follies

Shrapnel grazed his left heel.
No Achilles, Major Blake did not die,
but also didn't put in for another Purple Heart.
Ho Chi Minh flip flops

and running to the mess hall for ice
for our gin & tonic
during a rocket attack

in duty to the Drugstore.
Everyone knows tonic
helps stave off malaria.

Jack Crouchet

Military judge.
His courtroom, by God.

Far enough north that I had to take a C-130.
Packed in, scout dogs shitting,
Vietnamese soldiers puking,

then a convoy to a piece of shit tent courtroom.
You could tell the defendant.
The guy without a weapon.

The jury didn't want to be there.
They squirmed, anxious to get back to the field.
Counsel for both sides

rubbed our sweaty hands
on fatigue trousers, maybe took
a note or two.

The court reporter talked into a machine.
Malaria pills gave us all the shits.
"Convenience break, sir"

as we ran for the slit trench:
a foot on each board,
squatting.

So we try our case.
Some evidence, some argument, legalistic fiddle faddle,
then: We get hit.
Shouts of "incoming!"

But before we could get to the bunker
to return fire,
the prosecutor and I shoulder to shoulder,

he drawing from the hip, I from the shoulder,
LTC Jack Crouchet yelled "Recess!"

Because, after all, it was
his courtroom, by God.

Vung Tau

In Country R&R.
Room freezing from air conditioning,
fridge full of San Miguel beer.

Went to a bar,
paid Mama-San $15
for a young lady's company.

She wanted to go to the opera.
Music, singing, costumes
as bizarre as the chickens
running about, and rice popping.

Later, R&R Center,
Perry Mason on TV.
Then back to the separate chaos
of war.

Burning Ice Cubes

Just back from Tay Ninh, and my boss,
LTC Bob Jones,
told me to shower, get into clean jungle fatigues,
and meet him to burn an ice cube.

That was the deal:
One ice cube, a double shot of Jack.

I must have told my son.
Half century later,
in a place too pricey
we went to take a leak.
He said, "Let's burn a couple ice cubes."

In ritzy places they keep fresh ice in the urinals
so you won't smell piss.
We stood there, burning ice cubes,
always miraculously replaced.

Waiting for the Waiver Man

Not Xuan Loc,
nowhere near.

Presidio of San Francisco.
Real wooden desk courtrooms
and no incoming rockets or mortars.

And this:
the drive past the military cemetery
to the barracks of GIs

waiting to be boarded out.
Not serious enough for court martial,
but they could fight the board

or waive their rights,
take a general discharge—
less than honorable—lose some benefits.

One, a carnival worker by trade,
told me of his ring toss "joint"
and how he would sign anything
to get back to the carny:
"just waiting for the waiver man."

Drove past the cemetery on my way back.

Is there a waiver man?
We wait, all of us,
the best we can do.

Song of the Long Binh Jail

"Cuoi, Cuoi, the dream-time boy,
Alone, alone, on the moon"
　　—Vietnamese Folk Legend

You are hot on Christmas.
One of my boys smokes
aspirin in Camels

and the Commandant
says the only decorations
at Christmas in the Pacific

were Jap guts festooned across
barbed wire. The barbs themselves:
stars pricking a jungle roof.

In Silver City,
steel conex boxes,
heat sears me

and outside the gate
the sign: *No Pictures.*
No Walking This Side of Street.

Major, Sergeant Major

Major Ben knew that when you are in a firefight
and have cash,
of course you fall in love.

Ben had served in the British Army
before his 22 years
in the American forces.

And somehow, on leave in Hong Kong,
he fell crazy in love
with a whore named Betty Wong.

He brought artistic black and white photos
to the Officers Club.
Pretty girl.

The Army would discharge him
at the end of this tour.
No promotion or extension.

So if he couldn't be an officer,
he'd be a husband.
He'd find a job in Hong Kong.

And when he wasn't with her,
he'd find someone to listen to him talk
about Betty Wong.

Sergeant Major Monty
fell in love with Kim.
Local girl, worked on post.

Paid her, of course.
Occasionally he would show nude photos—
his Polaroid, no art to it.

Like Ben, the Army was letting him go.
Like Ben, he needed something.
And had cash.

We wonder what happened.
You have cash, fall in love,
and, as with the war itself,

nobody has answers,
no real ending to anything.

Morbidly Obese

Memorial Day Statistics:
Tom and I weigh a quarter ton
between us. Shoes on, of course.
Younger, trimmer friends have died.

Prime rib on the way to cemeteries
in Edison and Arapahoe.
Decorating the graves of our parents,
and the grandfather who successfully defended
his own brother in a murder case

and the great grandfather
wounded twice at Vicksburg
with Company A, 10th Iowa Infantry.

Tom and I are 165 years between us.
I try to remember the names
of fit young soldiers
in body bags in 1968-69.

Don't even know how many,
no names at all.

Silence

My final day in uniform.
The very last moment—
Presidio, San Francisco.

Polished floors,
chandeliers,
classic staircase.

And here's my job:
sign the registry book,
drop a copy of my orders through
the slot in the podium.

And I'm a civilian!
No handshake.
No *attaboy* backslap.

Nothing.
Took me days to clear post:
exit physical, paymaster, the works.

And now, nothing.
Almost like the moment by a body bag,
wondering if the Seiko watch

that poor kid had bought at the PX
was still there,
ticking.

Wondering if my silence was maybe
just a little
like his.

JB

I dreamt we chose to die a soldier's death.
Fiddler's Green charges us to empty our canteen
just as old Omar tells us to turn down an empty cup.

But Omar doesn't suggest the pistol, as Fiddler's Green
or my uncle Tunnard, whose German prisoners
made him art work for Christmas,
Signal Corps insignia from scraps of wood.
He accepted his Christmas gift by saluting his
prisoners, to their delight.
I have that small plaque in my den
but not the revolver he used to blow his brains out
slightly younger than we are,
going to a backyard picnic table, calling 911,
4 A.M. *Please no lights or sirens. I hope the gunshot
    won't wake the neighbors.*

Col Rheault wrote to me about a week before
he and his wife took their final walk, the day after
their anniversary, then she gently administered his
retreat.

We all break ranks.
That's the deal.
But tube feeding, diapers and bedpans, not what we
    signed up for, old soldier.

You ask to walk point on our last
patrol, but how do we do this?

Kipling suggests we roll to our rifle and blow
out our brains and go to our God like a soldier.

You and I started out cavalry.
The girl I left behind
will wear a yellow ribbon,
not black widow's weeds.

Gunga Dinh may be our water *bhisti*
but we'll sip from our canteen
amid the shades and shadows
on Fiddler's Green.

Fours

One of four kids, have four myself.
Earth, air, fire, water;
North, South, East, West,
Matthew, Mark, Luke, John,

the round earth's imagined corners,
as Donne says. The Fourth Amendment.
My deal. No unreasonable searches and seizures.
Your home, your castle. Pitt explained

the castle *may be frail— its roof may shake — the wind
may blow through it—the storm may enter—
the rain may enter—but the King of England
may not enter.*

So I huddled in that rice paddy. If I hunger
and thirst for righteousness,
I will be satisfied.
The Fourth Beatitude says so.

Prayer for My Child

not yet born

If not the stunning grace of unicorns,
These miracles as rare: At Gia Lai
A small boy walks on water. Who's to say
This miracle is lessened by the horns
Of that cool water buffalo beneath?
Insistent Presence, leave him room to pray!
Yet smartly field a thunderbolt gone stray,
And sometimes, at my father's grave, a wreath.

Let him move, as I move, through shatter-cane
In this Nebraska heat. Or murderous rain
In rice fields, under fire, alive and wry.
Or if a daughter, may You fortify
Her vision that she see both truth in thorns
And loveliness, more rare than unicorns.

PART 2
ONAWA

Lady Blanche

— For my mother, 1904-1974

What Speckled Band, what Greek Interpreter,
What Purloined Letter? And whose "blood to drink"?
You taught me mystery, led me to think
On evidence and clue, and to infer
Only such truth as lurks in crystal fact.

Now you are old, and of a distant age.
You hold, intense and still, to what you are,
Nor do you fear the waxing, spectral star
That takes you. And I still, therefore, my rage,
And give with love this book, this thought, this act

And anchor you, thereby, in time and space.
Remain in mastery. And go with grace.

Lady Blanche was the dedication poem for the collection of
Darkness of Snow, published by the Solo Press, 1973

Tommy

The town was Onawa.
Tommy, my best friend for 5 years,
before we both left Onawa, said it was the Dakota
word for Awake!

His mother was Sioux.
He spoke of Crazy Horse and Sitting Bull.
Loved the history and legends.

Years later, he told me my mother was the first
to serve him cake on a plate,
that my quarter horse Dixie was the first
        saddled horse he rode,

that my sister was the first person
        he ever saw play a piano,
except at school. He was a fast runner,
and a prankster.

One May Basket Day
he dressed as a girl, rang the bell, left a basket
and ran, knowing I couldn't catch him.

Tried to keep in touch.
He wanted to meet in Vegas.
Loved to gamble.

His cousin Wayne died.
Then his brother Robert. Then
I never heard from him again.

Animal

It doesn't matter how I got that name.
At age 13, there were worse.
It stuck.

Frank, palsied and shell shocked,
always leaning against Johnny's shoe repair,
called us slackers

and, against the wall in an alley,
the whittlers' bench. Behind the
courthouse, a park with a bandshell.

The high school band gave Thursday night concerts,
Bennie's dad sold nickel popcorn,
car horns applauded each number.

A month ago Dennis died, the last of the
"slackers gang," and there is no one left
to call me Animal.

M.Y.F.

I had it pretty good.
Front door in town,
back door in the country.

Had a horse and dog.
Our house was big enough
to entertain the Methodist Youth Fellowship.

Hawaiian Punch, cookies,
my mother or sister at the piano
as we sang popular songs before charades.

They all liked my folks,
the older sister who played the bassoon,
younger brother with his chemistry set.

Maybe that's why, after war and what it is,
I still agree with the friend who said *life is good,*
it oughtn't be any better.

Gut

Poor kid. Fat, but tough.
We called him "the rolling tackle."
Coach Bob told him to just hit the ground and roll.

A twist to our offensive line,
but it worked. At honors assembly
he got the D.A.R. history award.

Football coaches taught history.
Gut got a job, someone said,
as a gutter in the Sioux City stockyards.

Knew when his younger brother died,
a few years out of high school.
Don't know what happened to Gut,

but we all knew kids
whose lives never got better
after age 18.

Mutt

Big guy, good farmer, saw his wife
through the final cancer, taught his son
how to farm and do it right.

Once some hunters came on his land.
He put buckshot all over their trunk.
They complained; the sheriff told them

they were lucky it was their car,
not their butts. Mutt drove a truck of corn
into the elevator. Went into the bathroom,

dropped dead. A friend, dying of cancer,
said he envied Mutt
his perfect death.

Ray

My boxing coach was an old pug
once ranked by *Ring* magazine.

A bootlegger,
served good steaks,
had some gambling action.

When I fought a kid from the Reservation,
he told me the guy was too fast for me,
that I should tie him up and work on his ribs.

I won.
Never knew that the kid simply hadn't had
the luxury of my diet.

Ray was murdered
in a car.
The rules of bootlegging had changed.

My buddy Ralph took over some of his action,
        those years later.
I quit boxing.
My swimming coach told me to.

Tree Frog

Kid couldn't talk. Screamed. Small,
no harm to anyone.
Nobody minded,

nobody picked on him.
Didn't really sound like a tree frog—
just a scream. Kids were pretty good

at fitting him in, giving him a place.
One night he was walking home,
early evening. Some guy

had a grease fire; threw the pan
out the door
just as Tree Frog was passing.

They say the burning kid ran fast,
and his scream
was just like any normal burning kid.

Lonnie

Lonnie rode his bike.
Evenings, nights, alone,
his transistor radio always loud.

He came from some small town
in the Loess Hills where you can get lost,
among canyons and gullies and roads

you could never find again.
Skinny kid. Never saw him with anyone,
but he would pedal slowly, heading nowhere.

You could always hear his radio,
somehow a little like
Tree Frog's scream.

Jess

The night cop. In 1951,
if he was needed, the night phone operator
turned on the red light

atop the water tower. He would pick up a phone
and the operator told him the complaint.
One night a contractor was drunk and belligerent.

Jess pulled Gaylord over. Gaylord had his three dogs.
He told Jess he would go quietly,
but would not leave his dogs.

Jess wisely escorted Gaylord,
who had survived the Bataan death march,
home. Years later, Gaylord was dying in the hospital.

He left, decided to walk the few miles home.
Jess picked him up, drove him home,
where an old soldier has earned the right to die.

Walt

Years before I was his pall bearer,
he taught me to hunt, fish, fight,
ride and care for my horse.

He ought to know.
He had broken his back as a bull rider
in a rodeo. A semi pro baseball player,

he was foreman, then manager
at my dad's lumber yard.
I rode with him to his daughter's basketball game;

we passed a bottle back and forth.
He retired in Nebraska. I stopped by
and we drank too much whiskey in a bar.

Silver Star World War II, an old platoon sergeant,
he bragged that he got Christmas cards
from every man in his platoon.
That was the only brag he ever made.

Clara

Choir director and organist,
she filled the choir loft
with a few good singers.

Chuck Bachman became an operatic tenor.
Robed, we'd march down the aisle
The Lord is in his Holy Temple.

We looked good, I'm told.
Our star was the deep bass Bob,
a blind chiropractor.

He would hold my arm,
the way I hold a grandson's arm
when my cane isn't enough.

Our music was never recorded,
and a small picture of Clara hangs,
perhaps unseen, in the darkened robing room.

Alice

In her coffin, a lovely gown
that she had bought and saved
for that moment. Her eyes
had been blue as that gown.

Her father had told her
she must never marry,
must stay home and care for her mother,
and she did.

My brother and I would visit their tiny home,
wood-burning stove,
take the two of them driving
to see Christmas lights.

We would leave cookies
my mother had made
and wish them
a Merry Christmas.

Wilbur

Traumatic brain injury from a fall
kept him from completing Basic
in World War II,

but he was proud of being Infantry.
We worked together. Once his wife
tossed a candy bar into a truck,

he shared half, we made our delivery.
He was an usher in the Lutheran Church.
Some of the guys called him Humpty Dumpty

behind his back. Hard work, hot boxcars—
my brother and I bought him a gold watch
on his retirement. Loved the guy.

Shorty

He lived in outbuildings
wherever he found work.
Maybe never bathed,
but Rose married him.

She had a room above Sadie's café
where she did scut work.
Shorty said it was okay
but she had no teeth

and when she chewed tabaccy
it sounds like crickets, ya know?
Well, Shorty, we don't know,
but we can imagine.

Old Guys

He was in his 80s, and every July 4
he would swim the 300 yards across Blue Lake.
But he was nothing compared to Orrie.

Thanksgiving vacation, I was 14.
Orrie and I built a hog house from scraps around the
    lumberyard.
Ice crystals hung like rock salt in November air.

Orrie was an artist at work, in his 80s.
Homeric, I thought. Epic. Really something.
And my grandfather and uncle

practiced law into their 80s.
Old people don't know they are dying.
Or maybe they do.

Guys

Hoppy could beat any sophomore in the quarter mile.
Me, for sure. Divorced, not close to his son,
no grandkids, he came to Lincoln.

We drove to Whiting to see that his tombstone
had been properly placed next to those of his parents.
Then drove to see Boyd, Sarffie, and Ralph

all in different towns, all for the last time.
When we were 15, Ralph could pick up
a 50-pound sack of potatoes with his teeth,
then throw it over his shoulder.

He later owned a bar, needed a lawyer.
Hoppy was the last to die. I asked
to attend the burial of his ashes,
never heard back.

Girls

My mother had girl help.
Nita, Carolyn, and others.
Each a beauty, each friendly.

At 14, I shaved chin hair,
unloaded boxcars, swam, played second base.
I learned women at Blue Lake.

Julia sat on the dock, and pretty much
showed it all. Betty Jo was more subtle,
underwater, and intimate.

Years later I dated Carolyn.
Bosomy, a sweet summer.
Then many years later,

met her in a bar.
An open-mouthed kiss
months before cancer took her.

Pudge

Early in high school, he showed me my first
dirty picture. Nothing Julia hadn't shown us all,
but there was a guy, too.

Pudge liked to do his chores,
then ride his bike out to Blue Lake
to fish for bullhead at night.

Once some rich kids
thought it would be fun to turn out car lights
and speed along the grade.

Pudge was killed.
Half-assed investigation,
nothing done.

There are questions,
but now, after these years,
no one alive to answer them, a gift of
merciful irrelevance granted by death.

Ellen

"Nice young girl,
in a family way"
said Jonteel,

who liked to use her fingers
to count backwards,
from nine.

Bill didn't want to get married,
so Sheriff Whitmore picked him up,
drove him to Reverend Epps,

who married them.
Not shotgun, but
yeah, a Colt Police Special

was part of the uniform.
They stayed together,
married a half century

before Bill died,
then Ellen.

Susan

Her father was superintendent
of the Onawa Methodist Sunday School.
He signed my 1948 perfect attendance Bible.

Blonde, slender, knockout smile,
Larry fell in love with her.
Hell, we all did.

When Lana got polio,
Susan visited her at home daily,
bringing cheer, homework,
and prayer. Lana's mother told mine.

I heard Lana had a lovely funeral.
Anyway, college, then Larry proposed.
But: he had to say he accepted Jesus Christ as his
personal Lord and Savior.

Hell, Larry, just say it!
Nope, I'd have to keep on saying it.
She married someone else. He never married.

Saw her some years ago. Bad dose of cancer.
She smiled gently.
"I have my death sentence."

Trigger

She liked the Westerns.
Saturday afternoons, the Onawa Theater—
a nickel got you the serial, cartoon, and feature.

She wore jeans, western shirts, belts
and boots; affected a manly gait
and mannerisms, and nobody
ever found her pretty.

She made the mistake of claiming
to be related to Roy Rogers,
King of the Cowboys,

and from then on she was Trigger.
Lived out her life in Onawa,
perhaps content to be Trigger.

Charlotte

The male superintendent called an assembly.
Boys only. The woman who was principal
called one for girls.

Mr. Carpenter spoke of a case of
"venerable disease." Even if he had said it right,
we had no idea what he was talking about.

Charlotte had the clap. Must have been eighth grade
and her guy wasn't a student.
One case. She stayed in school

for a couple years, even attended a class reunion.
Some of the stories about her
may have been true. Certainly not all of them.

Maybe 20 years later, I saw her brother.
Ralph's bar. He grinned, said I should call her.
"You might get lucky."

Don

Always volunteering to coach
or referee. Backboard and yardlight
for shooting hoops. Smiling guy.

He drove the boys around.
Once, he took Danny under a bridge
and gnawed him.

Said if Danny told anyone he would kill
Danny's dad. But Danny couldn't pee.
His dad took him to the doc. *Who did this to you?*

Doc called Sheriff, who called Don, and
asked him to come in.
Don said sure, give him a little time to wash up.

Don drove out to the country,
hooked a hose from exhaust pipe to window.
Wrote a few notes. Died.

Nice tombstone in the cemetery.
People thanked the sheriff.
Excellent police work.

Frieda

She had been a "grand opera" singer, they said.
Married to the mayor, they owned Hotel Rivera.

Good fried chicken after church.
Coal heated rooms, fireplaces in each.

I would drive the truck,
carry scoops to each pullied basket,
my muddy boots and I outside.

She lived next door to Don.
Once she wouldn't give back a basketball
that landed in her flowers.

Don slapped her. My mother later said
that's when we should have known everything.

Flood

I am doing my dying work.
Gave a grandson my sword cane,
gave his brother a sports award.
Proper dying work

includes going through old boxes.
Baseball gloves, photos developed
in the old wine cellar I had turned into a dark room.

Pictures of my horse and dog,
beloved grandparents.
Then this: a photo of George Hudson with his spaniel,
signed *me and my dog.*

Then I remembered the flood of 1952.
We got to stay up late, sandbagging
the hospital. Drank coffee with
the engineers.

We were evacuated,
went to Sheldon, Iowa,
where my dad owned a lumberyard.
Reporters on motorboats, filming
Onawa,

7 miles in from the Raging Missouri.
Grain bins crushed like beer cans.
In Sheldon I fell in love,
backed down a bully,

became friends with George.
We each wrote a letter.
Some day I would look him up.
But he died in a car crash

before I said thanks,
or goodbye again.
A pattern for men my age
in the driest of years.

No Word

I have no one living here,
nobody buried in the cemetery.

I visit, a mere spectator,
combing the past alone.

Tommy taught me the word for Awake!
Nobody has taught me the word for death.

Sugar

World War 2 rationing books
left us a little short.
Matthew 24: wars and rumors of war.

Rumors of sugar, too.
Did Safeway really have marshmallows?
Someone had pre-war gum!

Saw my first bat
at my parents' Victory Garden.
We fattened a hog, Gravel Gertie.

For the families whose fathers were overseas,
my dad gave them coal for the winter,
sometimes a fruit basket for Christmas.

About looting:
Yes, it's true. Brits fight for Crown,
French for honor, Yanks for souvenirs.

My dad helped Freddie Johnson out.
Freddie had spent his lifetime hunting and trapping.
Once he found a bin full of bootleg whiskey.

He gave my dad a case of the best Scotch during
     Prohibition,
Dad gave him coal for his family all winter,
and sent him money before he shipped.

So, after the killing stopped, Freddie started a fight
in a bar. Threw ornately carved artillery casings
through the window. He picked them up in the alley,

brought them home for Dad. Milton Sloup
and his buddies ransacked a bar looking for steins.
What they found:
     a 100 pound bag of Great Western sugar—

Black Market, of course. Hope it brought those guys
a little sweetness, maybe a tender moment.
That's what you need, after war. Sweetness.

Valediction at the Lumberyard

— For my Father

Amid cement and lime
We bend to work; the hand,
With purpose, is the mind.
 By habit thus defined,
 Silent, we understand
Our common loss of time.

These buildings grew as you,
Knowing what was begun,
 Bent yourself to your thought;
 For here in what you wrought
Are marked what you have done
And what you plan to do.

These buildings will decay,
And you and they are old.
I could achieve this trade
and build with what you made;
by this I might withhold
the end you would delay.

But see me as your wraith;
Your death, but never you.
In looking, do not see
That which I would not be:
Submission were untrue
And not an act of faith.

For My Father on the Writing of His Will

GWB, 1898-1966

There was small sadness in this final act.
Giving was pleasure, even after death,
For you whose lasting faith outweighed the fact:
The tremble of your heart, your choking breath.

Bergie

R.B. 1941-2022

Phu Bai. We sat in the tower.
Tracers across the night.
Two Onawa guys,

talking Onawa guy stuff.
A couple months ago: dinner with our wives.
You gave me a 100 Piastre note.
That was the price on my head.
88 cents. Who said I'd never be worth a dime?

Last month: stroke. They found cancer.
Then coma. The familiar final wait.
We were young men on your family farm
where you grew up without indoor plumbing.

You saved soldiers who had been ground up
on Hamburger Hill. Went to Sweden to learn
your ancestral language. Took up the violin.

My parents welcomed you and Sheryl
during courtship. Your mother said
you weren't a real doctor, just a surgeon.

Will miss you, *bac si*.
And who's going to give me hydro morphine
to help me cross the river?

See ya, Bergie.
On the other side.

PART 3

PERSONAE

Brother to Dragons

RW (1936-2022)

You quoted Job.
The Omaha nation called you *Tenga Gahi*
Bull Buffalo Chief.

To the Pawnee you were
White Wolf/White Pawnee

Your Oglala Sioux name was
His Medicine Is Contrary

We were The Rog and Mad Dog.
We fought the good fight—mostly sober,
occasionally roaring drunk.

You came to our house to see the summit ash
Margaret and I planted the day you married Linda.

At a powwow you sat between us:
your cardiologist and me.
Said we had both saved your life!

And now I quote from Job:
"My harp also is turned to mourning."
And I join "the voice of them that weep."

Glenna

Girls, blonde as your teen years,
greeted you, sang Santa Lucia,
bringing morning light

and you owned Sweden
as you had owned Onawa,
playing your bassoon,

riding your horse,
you were a painter, a model,
and yes, a poet.

Both in our ninth decade,
I bet you could still scare hell
out of me,

telling ghost stories,
flickering the light switch ,
tapping on the gravestone

of the town cobbler.
And your smile
forever as sweet.

Marcia Southwick

The mind of rain
contemplates even the smallest crack in the parched dirt
where nothing will grow.
      —"The Rain's Marriage", Marcia Southwick

I was parched earth
to your Water Bride.

We watched our boys play football,
sipped at the VFW,
engaged the silent veterans.

Margaret and I
attended your wedding in Aspen
your horse drawn coach

heralded with mandolin.
Visited you and Murray
in Santa Fe.

Miles and years later
you are a gentle moment
for an old warhorse.

Bill Kloefkorn

1932-2011

The last time we met
you could no longer come
for Thursday morning
biscuits and gravy.

So I brought donuts to your house.
We talked about Pythagoras,
his "poets survive in fame"
notion, "more enduring than brass."

The belief that when we read and
understand,
the dead poet is alive in our minds.
I take down your books.
But first:

You loved
all things warm and breathing,
as you said. Poetry awards
meant less to you

than prizes for hog calling,
kite flying, and this contest:
country music titles!
The Hair on Her Chest is His

or *It's Lonely in the Saddle*
Since My Horse Died.
I think the winner was
You Are the Center Pivot
in the Sandhills of My Heart.

November 10 you celebrated
the Marine Corps Birthday
and you admitted you went to college
to play football. That was it.

Your basso profundo songs,
Why Did You Go to Broken Bow
And Leave Me Weeping Water?
And your audience would sing
Water in falsetto.

Loup River Expeditionary Force
sipping, singing, composing,
as you rafted the Loup,
grilling a steak or a catfish

and you were there with Rog and me
for Monastic Toasts of the Jacobins, Bastille Day.
On retirement, you sat in your rocker,
singing "Easy does it, easy does it."

I open a book.
Welcome back, Bill.

Gary Gabelhouse

1951-2019

Ice axe fight
on a mountain.
Your sixth degree black belt
and your powerful body

kept you here
to search the world
and write mystical thrillers.
On crutches, you came to my house.

The white silk scarf
you placed around my neck
was from the Dali Lama.
You have moved on

to whatever is or is not.

Ted Kooser

"If it were my poem..."
Then you fix it for me.

Old men,
"Heading for the Last Roundup"
 as Gene Autry sang in our youth.

You write every day.
Famous people brag that they know you.

But this memory: driving near your farm,
Margaret and I saw you and Kathleen in a ditch,
picking up beer cans and garbage.

Is that what poets do? Clean up after vandals?
Your quiet heroism takes me
where I no longer belong, don't want to go.

Still: thanks, Ted.

Wade Stevens

— *1896-1983*

56 years ago
you walked me through my first felony jury trial.
Henry wasn't too bright.
A successful paper hanger is more careful
with his checks.

The judge gave Henry 4 months
in the Hayes County Jail.
"You will get out in spring, when there is field work,"
Judge Westermaark said.

In January I asked Henry about Christmas in jail.
"Damn poor. But three hots and a cot."
I was hooked on the courtroom,
as you had once been.

You flew single seater in France
during World War I.
Coming back,
you bought a plane

for a local doctor.
Two big boxes off a boxcar.
A dray and draft horses hauled them
to a field where you and a mechanic

who had never seen a plane
put it together, and you flew it!
Proposed to your sweetheart, Aunt Flora,
in midair!

In 1919 you flew Doc Brewster
to Kansas for emergency surgery.
The first ever medical flight!
You landed in an alfalfa field,

a bedsheet hung from the windmill.
You stayed with the plane.
Cows would have eaten the banana-oiled
canvas on the plane.

Later, you prosecuted a KKK member
who had poisoned his wife.
A midnight exhumation,
the coffin welded shut.

The Klan killed your dog,
set your house on fire,
tried to kidnap your daughter.
Alfalfa John scared your cousin, Lilian Blanche.

You hung tough, sent him away for life.
Years later my daughter Laura shared
    a July birthday cake with you,
asked why your eyes were the color
    of your blue sweater,
and she delighted in your smile.

You were 87 when we lost you—
an age I approach,
thanking you again
for my first felony jury trial.

For Margaret

Uninterrupted water left me blind.
And blind, I wrote to you. The island rock
was less than color to the summer mind

where shadow blurred to sun and darkness. Blind,
therefore with stunning distance, I would write
too small for youthful moralists to find

one lie the gleaming hour had led me to.
To say, "You are not here. The waves are bright."
was facile, comfortless, but clearly true.

No matter. Love is something I recall
with shattering clarity beyond that rock.
Dark eyes, which in this moment encompass all.

Again: I'm sure the waves are bright and you
are still my love. The sun has seen us through.

Margaret's Family

In Sacred Heart Church,
Cedar Hills,
the heart of these "Bohemian Alps,"
the choir, a Czech funeral hymn.

Women wept,
for the passing of Frankie
and of their heritage.
Silver taps across the valley.

Frankie and his brother Milton—
Germany, World War II.
Milton was in a 4-storey
building, saw each floor destroyed,

ended up in a cellar, shattered wine bottles.
Captured during the Bulge,
went into a labor camp at 200 pounds,
was at 100 when a hometown cousin liberated him.

They stole a jeep and a bottle,
drove to the top of a hill,
drunk Bohemian farm boys.

And their sister, Rosalie,
stayed home, slopped hogs,
shocked corn, slaughtered chickens,
in their stead.

All married, had grandchildren, died.

Good life, good death.
Our sons are warriors.

Annie

On the Queen Mary,
crossing the Atlantic,
you were a student,

I was a brand new lawyer
accompanying my mother
on a trip my dad wouldn't take.

Years later you visited my mother
in Onawa. More years after that
we entertained you and John

in Onawa, though we have met
other places across the country.
Sometimes we speak of grandkids

or literature or politics.
Learning the varieties of love,
the forms of loss.

Brendan

Yes, young.
Dublin, 1961.
You and your brother Patrick

invited me home for tea.
You and I began our lifelong quest
for James Joyce.

Later our families met.
My mother gave your mother
a lovely blue scarf.

Music, discussions,
and yes, I gave you Onawa,

as you gave me Dublin.
Our friendship crosses the Atlantic,
as we have both done so often.

I am sure you would beat me at chess
and I would beat you at poker,
but friendship is never a game—
always a gift.

Henry Rothblatt

I practiced out of his Manhattan Office.
We represented celebrities,
also some people who were not nice.

Crowbars, broken knees, not nice at all.
In San Francisco, we kept a member
of the Grateful Dead out of the pen.

We went to a concert at Fillmore West,
we in suit and tie, on folding chairs.
Everyone else in jeans, on the floor.

He slept through the Dead concert.
A client who wrote *The Happy Hooker*
tried to bribe a cop.

Rothblatt said, "Never trust a whore."
I left New York. Henry sent us expensive gifts,
moved to Florida, wrote books, and died.

Brenda

Caught her singing in a bar.
She talked, sang of Vietnam.
Introduced myself.

She had been with the Taylor Sisters,
sang where they could, in-country.
Then, for years,

messages that must have seemed important
to her. Sent to me by someone
I didn't know.

Vietnam was a part of her mind,
her selfhood,
that didn't want to die.

Charlie

After Harvard,
he became a pediatric dentist
at a major hospital.

He treated only the hardest cases.
Perhaps a severe cleft palate.
He would tell frightened parents,

maybe fresh from El Salvador,
Your child is beautiful.
Say that. Tell me your child is beautiful,

and you must promise to tell that to your child
every day
to earn my treatment.

Then, Charlie would work his miracles.
Doing the Lord's work.

PART 4

MYTHOS

Atlas in Law School

Like a disease, my strength
(insistent as despair)
tightened the edge of where
I dared to be, until earth,
youth, and muscle fell
pressed to this Hercules:
eternal sophistries!
I reel in fear of hell,
dazed by my impotence,
uncertain of the truth.
My bout with turbulence
shall strangle yet my youth
but still my grip will stay.
And this was Lincoln's way.

Eros in the Orchard

The plums, red spheres against the naked sky,
Shake in the broken heat like rising fire.
The orchard shudders, as the wind comes high.

I come not quickly down in golden rain
when the plum tree is black against the sky
but leap forth, brute, from deep within the brain

and fade, not as seducer nor as sin,
but mindless sense, and as with golden rain
the air is sweeter where a god has been.

On Writing a Letter

It was the living mirror that they found:
Pygmalion and Narcissus, such as these;
The image binds desire, till, self-enwound,
The mind becomes the object that it sees.
The labyrinth of mirrors deceives the eye,
And one alone, aware of his duress,
Hears, strangled in his lust, Narcissus cry
Of broken ripples, chilled to nothingness.

I grope beyond the terror of this thought,
Seeking another's mind to release my own,
That my perception, past what sense has taught,
Becomes more than my image carved in stone.
And so I write, that through words I may find
The hard acceptance of another's mind.

Galatea: Pygmalion

I carved you from impassive stone.
Myself made woman. Here, alone,
I speak to you and hear my voice
Echo the exile of my choice.

Medusa Consoling Narcissus —
A Dialogue

True, you are dead, but think, when I was killed,
I also saw my image. You, self-willed,
stared at your own desire, slender and fair,
while I saw my crushed face and writhing hair.
I talked to none, and only heard the voice
of Gorgons. You, alone by selfish choice,
were never lonely. You saw your reflection
distorted by those ripples, but perfection
seemed constant there. Perception lost, you fell
too much into yourself. But here in hell
you suffer much, lamenting what you lost;
was not your love worth this, which is its cost?

II (his answer)

Perception lost? Strange words, Gorgon, from you
who petrified the vision, flesh, and mind
of all who chanced to see your face. You knew
my loneliness, and you were made as blind
as were your lovers, whom you now have met
unflinchingly. Perhaps you take some pride
in the indifference you cannot forget
even in hell, beside the men who died
from your impassive eyes and constant stare.
But I saw only one. I know the lust
for what is lost, for now my braided hair
has faded, and my lips and cheeks are dust.

III (her reply)

Patience. There is no passion here. My head
can never fix these shades. And you, instead
of faces, see in pools the faceless dead.

John Wayne

"I ain't got the words, ma'am"

Well, Duke, neither have I.
I'm tougher than you, you know.
Did in real life
what you did make-believe.
You made millions.
I got $65 a month combat pay.

So, though I ain't got the words,
how about if I just say
that she and I sometimes
think the same thing at the same time.

Close enough for me, Duke.

PART 5

DARKNESS OF SNOW

Darkness of Snow

Darkness of snow, cold moon on rifle stock;
Heavy in lethal silence, bright with sleet,
Trees shimmer, and the stirring birds repeat
The movement of the brittle leaves. The shock
Of slow wind, edging lifelessness to me
Quickens my stare into the snow that stills
Dark forms, that may be deer, on darker hills,
Increases, till I can no longer see.

My knowledge ends with visibility!
Snow fades on fresh, crystal tenacity
Lost against heat and blindness. When I turn
It is to blindness. Other snowflakes burn
New loss against me. I remain the same
In chill monotony of change: a name.

Stockville

Landlocked town, no paved roads leading in
or out, of course. County seat, courthouse,
center of justice.

Maybe the last wooden courthouse
in the country. Two outhouses.
One for men, one for the judge.

The judge's was a one-holer.
Local carpenter said, "Well, if it was a two-holer,
we figured by the time you decided where to sit,
you might have an accident."

County Judge kept the key to the courthouse
on a chain through a belt loop. People
waited around the flagpole for him.

One day he discovered the key and chain
weren't on his pants. He went home
and changed trousers.

During jury term, the Presbyterian ladies
from Curtis or Maywood brought lunch,
served it in the courthouse basement.

Long table for the men of the jury,
small tables for judge & court reporter,
and each side of the case.

Sally Cunningham sued, forced indoor plumbing
for herself, woman jurors, and others. A good lawyer,
she won. Center of justice, after all.

Big Bucks

Remember the tea time band
when I crossed the Atlantic
on the Queen Mary.

We passed the Queen Elizabeth.
Deck lights out; fog horn sounded
in a salute that was returned.

Sipped at the Wig & Pen Club,
400 year-old Staircase.
Another Queen Elizabeth

had ordered the club for journalists
and barristers outside the London walls,
spared them the fire.

Yale Club, Cornell & Stanford Club,
nice enough,
resort in Jamaica where our adult kids

learned the trapeze. Resort in Mexico
where our grandkids swam to their door.
No tipping, but I slipped the bartender

a few Cuban cigars. So what was the best?
Somehow, in III Corps I got to eat in the bunker
that was the General's Mess.

A legendary steak. The waiter, a lieutenant,
asked if I would like a second steak.
Hell yes! Damn straight! Luxury,

knowing that the next day
I would use my P-38 to open my C-rats,
earning my $65 a month combat pay.

Outage

Hurricane Henri's brute force hovers,
and I hope my friends have not lost power.

Waves can hit strong women
and hapless girls,

some guys seem okay at first.
Like a raft of explosives
floating down the Mekong,

and my lifeguard badge
can't help.
The waters that give us our lives
can fuck things up.

No Bob

After he died,
we met at a bar he owned.
Told stories.

I sat on what used to be
Mr. Pete's stool,
had my sip, bought a jar
for Mr. Pete,

as if that old soldier
and Bob were still around.

Havelock was a blue collar town
till Lincoln swallowed it.
Railroad folk.

Bob and Grace had a small bar and grill
that somehow grew into
a fine prime rib restaurant,

banners from the sport networks,
signed helmets from the Huskers
who had gone pro,

the best place to eat and drink
before Big Red games.
Pep bands, the works.

Dublin's Lord Mayor was a guest.
Corned beef and cabbage March 17;
over the bar a scull:

Myasis Dragon II.
Bob and Grace owned Havelock,
heart and soul,

and here we were in a smaller bar
they owned, across the street.
People asked

and I wouldn't tell.
About the boxes of rifles
addressed to Dublin

and found when that untitled house
in Havelock
exploded.

About the plaques in Gaelic.
Nope. Dunno.
We skipped the service,

Cathedral of the Risen Christ
where (we later learned)
the Bishop insisted that Mally Keelan

stand behind a screen to sing
Danny Boy.
So maybe God wouldn't see him?
Rumors of the hearse

passing by the bar.
We stood in the Autumn heat,
drinks in hand, but no hearse.
No Bob.

Hymn to Christ

On a November Evening

Thy blood burns suddenly.
Bright in the autumn mist
The night seems full of Thee
As if in Eucharist.

Tenuous is all grace
But pure intelligence.
Yet here Thy blessed face
Flickers, to permanence.

Ode to a Pinball Machine

We shift and pause
Helpless in laws
Of speed and weight.
And this is fate.

Bright numbers gloss
Our common loss.
The number scored
Is one's reward.

Love and the Plain Style

Praise lusty innocence.
Then studiously undo
False mystery with sense,
For sense is true.

Cultivate fair deceit.
Bastard of lust and chance,
Love dies or ripens sweet
In circumstance.

Speak of love's empty face,
But praise the cautious heart.
For much of love is grace
And much is art.

Sonnet from Mexico

Late afternoon, the wind, abrupt and cold,
Drives me to find a shelter; past dying birch
The broken road leads where the cross of gold
Stirs in the wind—here is the ancient church.
Inside the mission, artificial light
Leads me past frescoes, red with saints and hell:
Here to my left are candles, to my right
The brittle Christ of multicolored shell.

Against the walls He hovers everywhere.
His shadow, growing, turns with the lantern rope
Until I leave, and here in the still air
The neon-lighted Virgin of the Rose
Gives light to these few crumbling yards of slope
And fades to darkness, any way one goes.

August in Mexico, 1956

I. Church

Beyond the metal Christ, inside the door
I find the sanctuary. Here the floor
Is carpeted where supplicant pilgrims crawl
Toward the altar. Some, perhaps, recall
The years when they stood, as their children stand,
Outside the doors, too young to understand
The painted symbols, statues, carved wood, glass—
Asking forgiveness for these times, they pass
Carved benches, and move farther from the door.
Prayer comforts them, and helps them to ignore
The noises just beyond Christ's silver loins;
Their barefoot children, begging tourists' coins.

II. Brothel

I walk into the brown adobe house
And meet Alfredo, smiling, bald and thin.
He quickly leads me down the narrow hall
Until we reach the bedroom. We go in
And stand upon the cracked linoleum.
I find the yellow light above my head,
And turn it on, and see the stucco walls.
I see the one small window, and the bed—
Immense and covered with a gaudy spread.
There is a table, half-repaired by sticks,
And on it rest a mirror and a clock
And just above, a plastic crucifix.

III. Hospital Morgue, for the Unidentified Dead

Naked, the dead lie on concrete. Unknown,
Their flesh wastes here beneath the shadeless light.
The scalpel will turn flesh back from the bone;
No priest will come to give a final rite.

Letter of Thanks

— SJY and GRB

Alone again; the hallways of the heart
Nowhere have rooms to flee those hours that fell
Gorged with intent, but faceless, into hell.
Even the lies—confused, but not unkind—
Leave echoes. Friend, those echoes of the mind
Afford reflection. And from this comes art.

Valediction at Stanford

Class Poem, 1960

Though harsh and massive stone
Have held us here together,
We have remained apart,
Alike in lacking art,
Or wisdom, to atone
Much academic bother.

And much of this was waste.
Though brute unmeasured haste,
And inconclusive thought,
Suffice for who have sought
Some trivial social grace,
Or trade, leave not this place.

Content; O let the mind—
Incisive, querulous—
Be tough. The undefined
Yields slowly, yet men learn.
In knowledge, may we earn
Some shift from nothingness.

Of Sun and Moon

... our leap to God from fantasy
Is made in scorching hours...
— G.B.L.

If I shake down rude syllables from God,
They come in winter rain: my grinding skull
No kin to moon or sun, nor quick to cull
Divinity from rotting bush and pod.
Moon, icy witness to morality,
Gives shadow to the passing of the flesh,
And proves the instant. Must all bone enmesh
With earth and board, nor phase eternity!

The gleaming hours beneath the idiot sun
Belie the dissolution of the bone,
For fantasy to sleepiness must run
To lose the fact no sunlight may atone:
Insistent, Presence glitters in the brain.
The bitter grace of God. The winter rain.

Headstone

If someone killed the monster at Loch Ness
The monster's ghost swims the Australian crawl,
And frightened kids aren't comforted at all
That one ghost more comes from one monster less.
Take Raleigh's ghost. That poet-monster dead.
Was wont to ravish virgins in the tower.
Disadvantageous gesture! At an hour
When better judgment might have saved his head.

Ghost, random accident of monsters I
Shall choose to play, verse written, women loved
—and not in towers—warm accident allayed
And sickened by my waste, observe: I die.
Plead ignorance, not malice. Cheat all hell.

Ghost sprung from random monsters, wish me well.

Ecclesiastes

A time to die.

For sure.

A time to mend.

Maybe.

And finally

no time at all.

Before Thanksgiving

Ahead of the storm
we empty the garage.

She finds faded photos
stuck together, evidence
in a case I had forgotten.

Footprints
in a path
that no longer exists, though it once led
somewhere, a place that has also
disappeared.

Dead Man's Hand

A few more birthdays
and I'll draw a pair of eights.
Black aces in the hole.

Queen of Hearts in hand.
Surrounded by people I love
I will blow out the candle,

a chance to wish
if there were anything left
to wish.

The End

... the large gesture of solitary
man,
Resisting, by embracing, nothingness.
—Thom Gunn

Bob Rheault wrote me, "it's been a great ride"
a week or so before he died a warrior's death.

Commander of the Green Berets in Vietnam,
targeted to take the fall

for a CIA ordered assassination
of a double agent.

Marty, Bill, and I fought for him and his men,
got the charges dismissed.

My family stayed as Bob's guests at Owl's Head,
where Bob set up Outward Bound
for fellow vets.

He was our houseguest, spent a night
with old SEAL Bob Kerrey in the Governor's mansion.

The Green Beret case, my moment of history.
Of network TV. It fades as we die, all of us.

Lee Brumley and I met, our wives delighted,
in Houston and Galveston. Talked of travels,
soldiering, grandkids. A Chickasaw, he needed
no compass, navigated by the stars.

Cancer was taking him, but we sipped, ate,
good times, navigating by the stars.

Lee stayed in, transferred to Intelligence.
At the Pentagon, he met one of the CIA operatives,

who had lied under oath at our hearing.
The guy wanted to make up. Nope.

In England, attached to MI 6, he wore
his regimental tie: Blackhorse.

They all got smashed over lunch.
Wise Chickasaw, he never touched the stuff.

That same trip, saw my cousin Bob Berry,
"Sgt Guts" among the Chosin Frozen in Korea,
where he met Ted Williams!

Late 80s, he rode a Harley,
concealed carry, vodka from a tumbler.
Another last visit.

David Crew had written my mother that the Lord
had sent me to deliver him.

   He was an usher at our wedding.
He may be alive.

Margaret and I saw Budge Williams and his son,
somewhere in Georgia.

   Later Budge got back into trouble.
He may be dead.

Bill Hart and I defended a rape case at the Presidio
of San Francisco. Hippie chick picked up a young GI.
She thought they stripped down to sunbathe.
Bill was a judge when he died.

In Valhalla I will do courtroom battles,
always with Bill Hart and Marty Linsky.

Marty and Liz Linsky took me in when I was
between apartments in New York.
Liz once hosted us for Margaret's birthday.

Marty visited the Iowa farms,
appeared on my Lincoln radio show,
moved my admission to the U.S. Supremes
before retiring as a federal judge, and a colonel
in the reserves.

No hourglass, no compass.

I navigate by the stars,
guiding my journey to its end.

Publication Acknowledgements

The following poems were previously published in
Darkness of Snow (Solo Press, 1973):

"Lady Blanche"
"Darkness of Snow"
"Love and the Plain Style"
"Ode to a Pinball Machine"
"Valediction at Stanford"
"Sonnet from Mexico"
"August in Mexico"
"Valediction at the Lumberyard"
"For My Father on the Writing of His Will"
"Of Sun and Moon"
"Hymn to Christ"
"Headstone"

The following poem was previously published in
Those Gallant Men (Presidio Press, 1984):

"New Year's Eve, 1968"

The following poems were published in an anthology
issued by the Academy for American Poets and
edited by Louise Bogan:

"August in Mexico, 1956:
    I. Church
    II. Brothel
    III. Hospital Morgue, for the Unidentified Dead"